Whose home?

First published in Great Britain 1988
by Octopus Publishing Group for
The Parent and Child Programme
Published 1997 by Mammoth
an imprint of Reed International Books Limited
Michelin House, 81 Fulham Road, London, SW3 6RB
and Auckland, Melbourne, Singapore and Toronto

10 9 8 7 6 5 4 3 2 1

0 7497 3014 5

A CIP catalogue record for this title
is available from the British Library

Produced by Mandarin Offset Ltd
Printed and bound in Hong Kong

Whose home?

Written and devised by
David Bennett

Illustrated by
Julie Lacome

Here is a nest
high up in a tree.

Whose home can it be?

Do you know whose home it is?

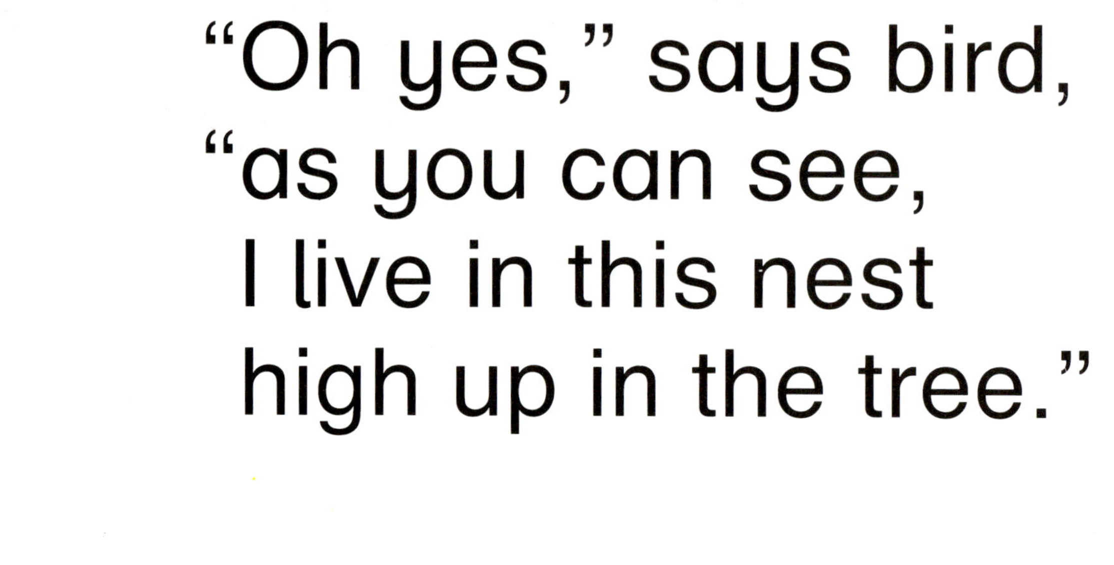

"Oh yes," says bird,
"as you can see,
I live in this nest
high up in the tree."

"Hello," says sheep,
"is it for me?"

"Oh no," says sheep,
"I live in a field."

"Hello," says hippo,
"is it for me?"

“Oh no,” says hippo,
“I live in a big river.”

"Hello," says spider,
"is it for me?"

"Oh no," says spider,
"I live in a web."

"Hello," says bear,
"is it for me?"

"Oh no," says bear,
"I live in a cave."

"Hello," says rabbit,
"is it for me?"

"Oh no," says rabbit,
"I live in a burrow."

"Hello," says snail,
"is it for me?"

"Oh no," says snail,
"I live in the shell
on my back."

"Hello," says baby,
"is it for me?"

"Oh no," says baby,
"I live in a house."

“Hello,” says frog,
“is it for me?”

"Oh no," says frog,
"I live in a pond."